Boss Chick Workbook & Goal Guide

Dr. Tangella Colston
CEO/Success Coach

Boss Chick Workbook & Goal Guide

iUniverse books may be ordered through booksellers or by contacting:

iUniverse
1663 Liberty Drive
Bloomington, IN 47403
www.iuniverse.com
1-800-Authors (1-800-288-4677)

Because of the dynamic nature of the Internet, any web addresses or links contained in this book may have changed since publication and may no longer be valid. The views expressed in this work are solely those of the author and do not necessarily reflect the views of the publisher, and the publisher hereby disclaims any responsibility for them.

Any people depicted in stock imagery provided by Getty Images are models, and such images are being used for illustrative purposes only.
Certain stock imagery © Getty Images.

ISBN: 978-1-5320-7151-5 (sc)
ISBN: 978-1-5320-7152-2 (e)

Print information available on the last page.

iUniverse rev. date: 03/27/2019

About the Author

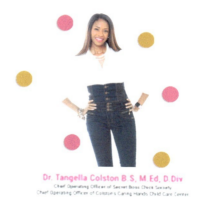

Dr. Tangella Colston B.S, M.Ed, D.Div
Chief Operating Officer of Secret Boss Chick Society
Chief Operating Officer of Colston's Caring Hands Child Care Center

Tangella grew up in Highland Park, Michigan and has always had the desire to help empower, encourage and empower people in life and on their spiritual journey. She is a mother of 3 children, a wife of over 10 years, an ordained Minister and the CEO of two successful businesses. Her desire has always been to have complete financial freedom by having 7 sources of incomes. She has been an entrepreneur for 10 years with a Bachelors of Science Degree from Michigan State University in Family & Community Services with an emphasis in Administration Early Childhood Programs and a Masters of Arts Degree in Early Childhood Education from Oakland University. She had a vision to start a daycare and started it out her home in 2009. She was always full and God forced her to expand her vison! After 5 years she opened her center in Madison Heights, Michigan without any money, savings and with a low credit score. She named her daycare Colston's Caring Hands Child Care so that she could leave a legacy for her children the daycare was built from the ground up where she drew, designed and created the perfect image of a dream come true her own child care facility. With in 1 year the business was completely full and she was forced again to expand and doubled capacity again fully enrolled within 5 weeks. In just 3 years she managed to expand 3 times.

Childcare has always been her dream but people is her ministry. In December 2016 Right before graduating Ministry school in June 2017 she prayed and asked God to birth her Ministry and Secret Boss Chick Society was Born. It started with five members (Angela Merriweather, Zatavia Berry, Chemeeker Waller, Latavia Vance and Tangella Colston) in less than 3 months' membership grew to 56 members and lives were completely changed. The goal was to encourage, empower and encourage women in every area of their life. Over 14 members started businesses and 5 additional left their jobs within the first year under the mentorship and support of Dr. Colstons' leadership.

Contents

Boss Rule # 1
DEFINE YOUR INTEREST & PURPOSE 1

Boss Rule # 2
CREATING A PERSONAL MISSION STATEMENT 2

Boss Rule # 3
REDEFINING YOUR MINDSET 4

Boss Rule # 4
ESTABLISHING YOUR GOALS 6

Boss Rule # 5
DOMINATING MONEY TO SUPPORT YOUR GOALS 193

Boss Rule # 6
GOAL DIGGIN 206

Boss Rule # 1
DEFINE YOUR INTEREST & PURPOSE

"The meaning of life is to find your gift
And the purpose of life is to give it away"

Key: Try to answer the questions in no longer than 1 minute or less

1. What use to make you happy as a child?
2. If you had 24 hours to do something you love what would it be?
3. What is your talent?
4. What is one thing that you would do for free just because you enjoy it?
5. What is your gift?
6. What makes you smile? (Activities, people, hobbies, interest…)
7. What activities make you lose track of time?
8. What makes you feel good about yourself?
9. Who Inspires you?
10. Why does this person inspire you?
11. What skills, activities, gifts do you have and can display with little to no effort?
12. Is there something people often ask you to do or ask for help with?
13. Name at least three hardships that you have had to overcome?
    1.
    2.
    3.

14. What was the process for overcoming hardships?

Boss Rule # 2
CREATING A PERSONAL MISSION STATEMENT

"Your personal mission statement becomes the
DNA for every other decision you make"

The words you speak manifest and start to take over your thoughts so it is very important to develop a positive personal mission statement that you can often reflect on or use as a reminder to stay on a positive road.

Mission statements can also help you stay on task and be a reminder of your personal goals. It is a great idea to write them down and stick them on your mirror or next to your bed.

It is important to live in purpose and in passion. Developing a personal mission statement will remind you of what your purpose is and how to complete it with consistent passion.

The difference between doing something you like and love is that what you love you would often do for free. When you operate in passion that is what sets you aside from other people who have just a job or a successful career.

Purpose is who you are when you are able to live FREE from worry, being fearful, or being protective of showing people the real you. It is the Authentic YOU!

Your life Purpose is something you can't fail to be as long as you align yourself with passion.

The key to success is consistency

Your mission statement should be short and answer these three short questions:

Words that you can use:

Educate   Accomplish   Empower

Encourage   Improve   Help   Give

Guide   Inspire   Master   Motivate

Nurture   Organize   Produce

Promote   Share   Understand

What do I want to do?

_____

_____

_____

Who do I want to help?

_____

_____

_____

What will the result be or what values will I create? What problem will I solve?

_____

_____

_____

Boss Rule # 3
REDEFINING YOUR MINDSET

"Every BOSS started out as a worker"

"Change your mind and you will change your life"

Every Successful person in life or in business have to develop goals

But before you develop goals you must examine your habits. Redefining your mindset starts with developing Positive Habits so lets start by:

List some of your Bad Habits

_____

_____

_____

_____

List some things you have been putting off

_____

_____

_____

Why have you been putting these things off?

_____

_____

_____

Boss Rule # 4
ESTABLISHING YOUR GOALS

"A Goal without a Plan is just a Wish"

Goal Planning Guide

What is a Goal Newsletter?

Goal Overview

List Each Goal under Topic and underneath start naming
what you need to do to get started with this goal

Goal Tracker Plan Sheet

Analyze each goal by doing a Tracker Planner Sheet for each Goal

Calendar

Weekly Goal Digger Tracker

Weekly priorities:

Go to your Goal Overview sheet and List at least 1 thing to do from each one of your
Goal Overview list under each topic and write them under your weekly priorities

Weekly Checklist:

Write places you need to go, people you need to call or things you need to buy

Notes:

This tab can be used to write down phone numbers, websites,
email addresses or other important information

Days of the week – Weekly Goal Tracker

Use your Checklist and write in the things you need to do on one of the days of the week and continue until you write down every priority on a day. You should focus on doing a realistic amount of goals per day.

Weekly Schedule Guide

Use the Weekly Goal Digger Tracker and break down each day by writing in what time you plan on doing your daily obligations. It is important to put in travel time, meal times and prep and locations. You can also block off times to make phone calls and etc. This part is extremely important because it sets the tone for your Goal that you need to focus on each day as well as keeping you discipline with prioritizing your time.

Sunday	Monday	Tuesday	Wednesday	Thursday	Friday	Saturday

Goal Digger Workbook

Goal Overview

List Each Goal under Topic and underneath start naming what you need to do to get started with this goal

Goal	
Topic	
🔗	
🔗	
🔗	
🔗	
Time Frame	How many months to accomplish?
Reward	

Goal	
Topic	
🔗	
🔗	
🔗	
🔗	
Time Frame	How many months to accomplish?
Reward	

Analyze each goal by doing a Tracker Planner Sheet for each Goal

GOAL TRACKER PLAN SHEET

Goal:

Motivation/Reward:

Start Date: _____ Goal Completion Date: _____

Duration? How long will it take? _____

ACTION PLAN

STEPS NEEDED TO COMPLETE GOAL:

Anticipated Completion Date:

Possible Road Blocks:

Analyze each goal by doing a Tracker Planner Sheet for each Goal

GOAL TRACKER PLAN SHEET

Goal :

Motivation/Reward:

Start Date: _____   Goal Completion Date: _____

Duration? How long will it take? _____

ACTION PLAN

STEPS NEEDED TO COMPLETE GOAL:

Anticipated Completion Date:

Possible Road Blocks:

WEEKLY GOAL DIGGER TRACKER

Weekly priorities:

Go to your Goal Overview sheet and List at least 1 thing to do from each one of your
Goal Overview list under each topic and write them under your weekly priorities

Weekly Priorities:

Weekly Checklist:

Write places you need to go, people you need to call or things you need to buy

Weekly Checklist:

Notes:

This tab can be used to write down phone numbers, websites,
email addresses or other important information

WEEKLY GOAL DIGGER TRACKER

Use your Checklist and write in the things you need to do on one of the days of the week and continue until you write down every priority on a day. You should focus on doing a realistic amount of goals per day.

Week:

Monday

Tuesday

Wednesday

Thursday

Friday

Saturday

Sunday

- Use the Weekly Goal Digger Tracker and break down each day by writing in what time you plan on doing your daily obligations. It is important to put in travel time, meal times and prep and locations. You can also block off times to make phone calls and etc. This part is extremely important because it sets the tone for your Goal that you need to focus on each day as well as keeping you discipline with prioritizing your time.

	Monday	Tuesday	Wednesday	Thursday	Friday	Saturday	Sunday
6:30am							
7:00am							
7:30am							
8:00am							
8:30am							
9:00am							
9:30am							
10:00am							
10:30am							
11:00am							
11:30am							
12:00pm							
12:30pm							
1:00pm							
1:30pm							
2:00pm							
2:30pm							
3:00pm							
3:30pm							
4:00pm							

	Monday	Tuesday	Wednesday	Thursday	Friday	Saturday	Sunday
4:30pm							
5:00pm							
5:30pm							
6:00pm							
6:30pm							
7:00pm							
7:30pm							
8:00pm							
8:30pm							
9:00pm							
9:30pm							
10:00pm							
10:30pm							

BOSS CHICK

GOAL TRACKER PLAN SHEET

Goal :

Motivation/Reward:

Start Date: _____ Goal Completion Date: _____

Duration? How long will it take? _____

ACTION PLAN

STEPS NEEDED TO COMPLETE GOAL:

Anticipated Completion Date:

Possible Road Blocks:

WEEKLY GOAL DIGGER TRACKER

Weekly priorities:

Go to your Goal Overview sheet and List at least 1 thing to do from each one of your Goal Overview list under each topic and write them under your weekly priorities

Weekly Priorities:

Weekly Checklist:

Write places you need to go, people you need to call or things you need to buy

Weekly Checklist:

Notes:

This tab can be used to write down phone numbers, websites, email addresses or other important information

WEEKLY GOAL DIGGER TRACKER

Week

Monday

Tuesday

Wednesday

Thursday

Friday

Saturday

Sunday

	Monday	Tuesday	Wednesday	Thursday	Friday	Saturday	Sunday
6:30am							
7:00am							
7:30am							
8:00am							
8:30am							
9:00am							
9:30am							
10:00am							
10:30am							
11:00am							
11:30am							
12:00pm							
12:30pm							
1:00pm							
1:30pm							
2:00pm							
2:30pm							
3:00pm							
3:30pm							
4:00pm							
4:30pm							
5:00pm							
5:30pm							
6:00pm							

	Monday	Tuesday	Wednesday	Thursday	Friday	Saturday	Sunday
6:30pm							
7:00pm							
7:30pm							
8:00pm							
8:30pm							
9:00pm							
9:30pm							
10:00pm							
10:30pm							

GOAL TRACKER PLAN SHEET

Goal:

Motivation/Reward:

Start Date: _____ Goal Completion Date: _____

Duration? How long will it take? _____

ACTION PLAN

STEPS NEEDED TO COMPLETE GOAL:

Anticipated Completion Date:

Possible Road Blocks:

WEEKLY GOAL DIGGER TRACKER

Weekly Priorities:

Weekly Checklist:

Notes:

WEEKLY GOAL DIGGER TRACKER

Week	
Monday	
Tuesday	
Wednesday	
Thursday	
Friday	
Saturday	
Sunday	

	Monday	Tuesday	Wednesday	Thursday	Friday	Saturday	Sunday
6:30am							
7:00am							
7:30am							
8:00am							
8:30am							
9:00am							
9:30am							
10:00am							
10:30am							
11:00am							
11:30am							
12:00pm							
12:30pm							
1:00pm							
1:30pm							
2:00pm							
2:30pm							
3:00pm							
3:30pm							
4:00pm							
4:30pm							
5:00pm							
5:30pm							
6:00pm							

	Monday	Tuesday	Wednesday	Thursday	Friday	Saturday	Sunday
6:30pm							
7:00pm							
7:30pm							
8:00pm							
8:30pm							
9:00pm							
9:30pm							
10:00pm							
10:30pm							

BOSS CHICK

GOAL TRACKER PLAN SHEET

Goal:

Motivation/Reward:

Start Date: _____   Goal Completion Date: _____

Duration? How long will it take? _____

ACTION PLAN

STEPS NEEDED TO COMPLETE GOAL:

Anticipated Completion Date:

Possible Road Blocks:

WEEKLY GOAL DIGGER TRACKER

Weekly Priorities:

Weekly Checklist:

Notes:

WEEKLY GOAL DIGGER TRACKER

Week

Monday

Tuesday

Wednesday

Thursday

Friday

Saturday

Sunday

	Monday	Tuesday	Wednesday	Thursday	Friday	Saturday	Sunday
6:30am							
7:00am							
7:30am							
8:00am							
8:30am							
9:00am							
9:30am							
10:00am							
10:30am							
11:00am							
11:30am							
12:00pm							
12:30pm							
1:00pm							
1:30pm							
2:00pm							
2:30pm							
3:00pm							
3:30pm							
4:00pm							
4:30pm							
5:00pm							
5:30pm							
6:00pm							

	Monday	Tuesday	Wednesday	Thursday	Friday	Saturday	Sunday
6:30pm							
7:00pm							
7:30pm							
8:00pm							
8:30pm							
9:00pm							
9:30pm							
10:00pm							
10:30pm							

Sunday	Monday	Tuesday	Wednesday	Thursday	Friday	Saturday

Goal Digger Workbook

Goal Overview

Analyze each goal by doing a Tracker Planner Sheet for each Goal

---

GOAL TRACKER PLAN SHEET

Goal :

Motivation/Reward:

Start Date: _____ Goal Completion Date: _____

Duration? How long will it take? _____

ACTION PLAN

STEPS NEEDED TO COMPLETE GOAL:

Anticipated Completion Date:

Possible Road Blocks:

Analyze each goal by doing a Tracker Planner Sheet for each Goal

GOAL TRACKER PLAN SHEET

Goal:

Motivation/Reward:

Start Date: _____   Goal Completion Date: _____

Duration? How long will it take? _____

ACTION PLAN

STEPS NEEDED TO COMPLETE GOAL:

Anticipated Completion Date:

Possible Road Blocks:

GOAL TRACKER PLAN SHEET

Goal :

Motivation/Reward:

Start Date: _____   Goal Completion Date: _____

Duration? How long will it take? _____

ACTION PLAN

STEPS NEEDED TO COMPLETE GOAL:

Anticipated Completion Date:

Possible Road Blocks:

WEEKLY GOAL DIGGER TRACKER

Weekly Priorities:

Weekly Checklist:

Notes:

WEEKLY GOAL DIGGER TRACKER

Week

Monday

Tuesday

Wednesday

Thursday

Friday

Saturday

Sunday

	Monday	Tuesday	Wednesday	Thursday	Friday	Saturday	Sunday
6:30am							
7:00am							
7:30am							
8:00am							
8:30am							
9:00am							
9:30am							
10:00am							
10:30am							
11:00am							
11:30am							
12:00pm							
12:30pm							
1:00pm							
1:30pm							
2:00pm							
2:30pm							
3:00pm							
3:30pm							
4:00pm							
4:30pm							
5:00pm							
5:30pm							
6:00pm							

	Monday	Tuesday	Wednesday	Thursday	Friday	Saturday	Sunday
6:30pm							
7:00pm							
7:30pm							
8:00pm							
8:30pm							
9:00pm							
9:30pm							
10:00pm							
10:30pm							

GOAL TRACKER PLAN SHEET

Goal :

Motivation/Reward:

Start Date: _____ Goal Completion Date: _____

Duration? How long will it take? _____

ACTION PLAN

STEPS NEEDED TO COMPLETE GOAL:

Anticipated Completion Date:

Possible Road Blocks:

WEEKLY GOAL DIGGER TRACKER

Weekly Priorities:

Weekly Checklist:

Notes:

WEEKLY GOAL DIGGER TRACKER

Week

Monday

Tuesday

Wednesday

Thursday

Friday

Saturday

Sunday

	Monday	Tuesday	Wednesday	Thursday	Friday	Saturday	Sunday
6:30am							
7:00am							
7:30am							
8:00am							
8:30am							
9:00am							
9:30am							
10:00am							
10:30am							
11:00am							
11:30am							
12:00pm							
12:30pm							
1:00pm							
1:30pm							
2:00pm							
2:30pm							
3:00pm							
3:30pm							
4:00pm							
4:30pm							
5:00pm							
5:30pm							
6:00pm							

	Monday	Tuesday	Wednesday	Thursday	Friday	Saturday	Sunday
6:30pm							
7:00pm							
7:30pm							
8:00pm							
8:30pm							
9:00pm							
9:30pm							
10:00pm							
10:30pm							

BOSS CHICK

GOAL TRACKER PLAN SHEET

Goal :

Motivation/Reward:

Start Date: _____ Goal Completion Date: _____

Duration? How long will it take? _____

ACTION PLAN

STEPS NEEDED TO COMPLETE GOAL:

Anticipated Completion Date:

Possible Road Blocks:

WEEKLY GOAL DIGGER TRACKER

Weekly Priorities:

Weekly Checklist:

Notes:

WEEKLY GOAL DIGGER TRACKER

Week

Monday

Tuesday

Wednesday

Thursday

Friday

Saturday

Sunday

	Monday	Tuesday	Wednesday	Thursday	Friday	Saturday	Sunday
6:30am							
7:00am							
7:30am							
8:00am							
8:30am							
9:00am							
9:30am							
10:00am							
10:30am							
11:00am							
11:30am							
12:00pm							
12:30pm							
1:00pm							
1:30pm							
2:00pm							
2:30pm							
3:00pm							
3:30pm							
4:00pm							
4:30pm							
5:00pm							
5:30pm							
6:00pm							

	Monday	Tuesday	Wednesday	Thursday	Friday	Saturday	Sunday
6:30pm							
7:00pm							
7:30pm							
8:00pm							
8:30pm							
9:00pm							
9:30pm							
10:00pm							
10:30pm							

GOAL TRACKER PLAN SHEET

Goal:

Motivation/Reward:

Start Date: _____ Goal Completion Date: _____

Duration? How long will it take? _____

ACTION PLAN

STEPS NEEDED TO COMPLETE GOAL:

Anticipated Completion Date:

Possible Road Blocks:

WEEKLY GOAL DIGGER TRACKER

Weekly Priorities:

Weekly Checklist:

Notes:

WEEKLY GOAL DIGGER TRACKER

Week	
Monday	
Tuesday	
Wednesday	
Thursday	
Friday	
Saturday	
Sunday	

	Monday	Tuesday	Wednesday	Thursday	Friday	Saturday	Sunday
6:30am							
7:00am							
7:30am							
8:00am							
8:30am							
9:00am							
9:30am							
10:00am							
10:30am							
11:00am							
11:30am							
12:00pm							
12:30pm							
1:00pm							
1:30pm							
2:00pm							
2:30pm							
3:00pm							
3:30pm							
4:00pm							
4:30pm							
5:00pm							
5:30pm							
6:00pm							

	Monday	Tuesday	Wednesday	Thursday	Friday	Saturday	Sunday
6:30pm							
7:00pm							
7:30pm							
8:00pm							
8:30pm							
9:00pm							
9:30pm							
10:00pm							
10:30pm							

Sunday	Monday	Tuesday	Wednesday	Thursday	Friday	Saturday

Goal Digger Workbook

Goal Overview

Analyze each goal by doing a Tracker Planner Sheet for each Goal

GOAL TRACKER PLAN SHEET

Goal:

Motivation/Reward:

Start Date: _____ Goal Completion Date: _____

Duration? How long will it take? _____

ACTION PLAN

STEPS NEEDED TO COMPLETE GOAL:

Anticipated Completion Date:

Possible Road Blocks:

Analyze each goal by doing a Tracker Planner Sheet for each Goal

GOAL TRACKER PLAN SHEET

Goal :

Motivation/Reward:

Start Date: _____ Goal Completion Date: _____

Duration? How long will it take? _____

ACTION PLAN

STEPS NEEDED TO COMPLETE GOAL:

Anticipated Completion Date:

Possible Road Blocks:

GOAL TRACKER PLAN SHEET

Goal :

Motivation/Reward:

Start Date: _____ Goal Completion Date: _____

Duration? How long will it take? _____

ACTION PLAN

STEPS NEEDED TO COMPLETE GOAL:

Anticipated Completion Date:

Possible Road Blocks:

WEEKLY GOAL DIGGER TRACKER

Weekly Priorities:

Weekly Checklist:

Notes:

WEEKLY GOAL DIGGER TRACKER

Week

Monday

Tuesday

Wednesday

Thursday

Friday

Saturday

Sunday

	Monday	Tuesday	Wednesday	Thursday	Friday	Saturday	Sunday
6:30am							
7:00am							
7:30am							
8:00am							
8:30am							
9:00am							
9:30am							
10:00am							
10:30am							
11:00am							
11:30am							
12:00pm							
12:30pm							
1:00pm							
1:30pm							
2:00pm							
2:30pm							
3:00pm							
3:30pm							
4:00pm							
4:30pm							
5:00pm							
5:30pm							
6:00pm							

	Monday	Tuesday	Wednesday	Thursday	Friday	Saturday	Sunday
6:30pm							
7:00pm							
7:30pm							
8:00pm							
8:30pm							
9:00pm							
9:30pm							
10:00pm							
10:30pm							

GOAL TRACKER PLAN SHEET

Goal :

Motivation/Reward:

Start Date: _____ Goal Completion Date: _____

Duration? How long will it take? _____

ACTION PLAN

STEPS NEEDED TO COMPLETE GOAL:

Anticipated Completion Date:

Possible Road Blocks:

WEEKLY GOAL DIGGER TRACKER

Weekly Priorities:

Weekly Checklist:

Notes:

WEEKLY GOAL DIGGER TRACKER

Week

Monday

Tuesday

Wednesday

Thursday

Friday

Saturday

Sunday

	Monday	Tuesday	Wednesday	Thursday	Friday	Saturday	Sunday
6:30am							
7:00am							
7:30am							
8:00am							
8:30am							
9:00am							
9:30am							
10:00am							
10:30am							
11:00am							
11:30am							
12:00pm							
12:30pm							
1:00pm							
1:30pm							
2:00pm							
2:30pm							
3:00pm							
3:30pm							
4:00pm							
4:30pm							
5:00pm							
5:30pm							
6:00pm							

	Monday	Tuesday	Wednesday	Thursday	Friday	Saturday	Sunday
6:30pm							
7:00pm							
7:30pm							
8:00pm							
8:30pm							
9:00pm							
9:30pm							
10:00pm							
10:30pm							

GOAL TRACKER PLAN SHEET

Goal:

Motivation/Reward:

Start Date: _____ Goal Completion Date: _____

Duration? How long will it take? _____

ACTION PLAN

STEPS NEEDED TO COMPLETE GOAL:

Anticipated Completion Date:

Possible Road Blocks:

WEEKLY GOAL DIGGER TRACKER

Weekly Priorities:

Weekly Checklist:

Notes:

WEEKLY GOAL DIGGER TRACKER

Week

Monday

Tuesday

Wednesday

Thursday

Friday

Saturday

Sunday

	Monday	Tuesday	Wednesday	Thursday	Friday	Saturday	Sunday
6:30am							
7:00am							
7:30am							
8:00am							
8:30am							
9:00am							
9:30am							
10:00am							
10:30am							
11:00am							
11:30am							
12:00pm							
12:30pm							
1:00pm							
1:30pm							
2:00pm							
2:30pm							
3:00pm							
3:30pm							
4:00pm							
4:30pm							
5:00pm							
5:30pm							
6:00pm							

	Monday	Tuesday	Wednesday	Thursday	Friday	Saturday	Sunday
6:30pm							
7:00pm							
7:30pm							
8:00pm							
8:30pm							
9:00pm							
9:30pm							
10:00pm							
10:30pm							

GOAL TRACKER PLAN SHEET

Goal :

Motivation/Reward:

Start Date: _____   Goal Completion Date: _____

Duration? How long will it take? _____

ACTION PLAN

STEPS NEEDED TO COMPLETE GOAL:

Anticipated Completion Date:

Possible Road Blocks:

WEEKLY GOAL DIGGER TRACKER

Weekly Priorities:

Weekly Checklist:

Notes:

WEEKLY GOAL DIGGER TRACKER

Week

Monday

Tuesday

Wednesday

Thursday

Friday

Saturday

Sunday

	Monday	Tuesday	Wednesday	Thursday	Friday	Saturday	Sunday
6:30am							
7:00am							
7:30am							
8:00am							
8:30am							
9:00am							
9:30am							
10:00am							
10:30am							
11:00am							
11:30am							
12:00pm							
12:30pm							
1:00pm							
1:30pm							
2:00pm							
2:30pm							
3:00pm							
3:30pm							
4:00pm							
4:30pm							
5:00pm							
5:30pm							
6:00pm							

	Monday	Tuesday	Wednesday	Thursday	Friday	Saturday	Sunday
6:30pm							
7:00pm							
7:30pm							
8:00pm							
8:30pm							
9:00pm							
9:30pm							
10:00pm							
10:30pm							

Sunday	Monday	Tuesday	Wednesday	Thursday	Friday	Saturday

Goal Digger Workbook

Goal Overview

Analyze each goal by doing a Tracker Planner Sheet for each Goal

GOAL TRACKER PLAN SHEET

Goal :

Motivation/Reward:

Start Date: _____ Goal Completion Date: _____

Duration? How long will it take? _____

ACTION PLAN

STEPS NEEDED TO COMPLETE GOAL:

Anticipated Completion Date:

Possible Road Blocks:

Analyze each goal by doing a Tracker Planner Sheet for each Goal

GOAL TRACKER PLAN SHEET

Goal:

Motivation/Reward:

Start Date: _____   Goal Completion Date: _____

Duration? How long will it take? _____

ACTION PLAN

STEPS NEEDED TO COMPLETE GOAL:

Anticipated Completion Date:

Possible Road Blocks:

GOAL TRACKER PLAN SHEET

Goal :

Motivation/Reward:

Start Date: _____   Goal Completion Date: _____

Duration? How long will it take? _____

ACTION PLAN

STEPS NEEDED TO COMPLETE GOAL:

Anticipated Completion Date:

Possible Road Blocks:

WEEKLY GOAL DIGGER TRACKER

Weekly Priorities:

Weekly Checklist:

Notes:

WEEKLY GOAL DIGGER TRACKER

Week

Monday

Tuesday

Wednesday

Thursday

Friday

Saturday

Sunday

	Monday	Tuesday	Wednesday	Thursday	Friday	Saturday	Sunday
6:30am							
7:00am							
7:30am							
8:00am							
8:30am							
9:00am							
9:30am							
10:00am							
10:30am							
11:00am							
11:30am							
12:00pm							
12:30pm							
1:00pm							
1:30pm							
2:00pm							
2:30pm							
3:00pm							
3:30pm							
4:00pm							
4:30pm							
5:00pm							
5:30pm							
6:00pm							

	Monday	Tuesday	Wednesday	Thursday	Friday	Saturday	Sunday
6:30pm							
7:00pm							
7:30pm							
8:00pm							
8:30pm							
9:00pm							
9:30pm							
10:00pm							
10:30pm							

GOAL TRACKER PLAN SHEET

Goal:

Motivation/Reward:

Start Date: _____ Goal Completion Date: _____

Duration? How long will it take? _____

ACTION PLAN

STEPS NEEDED TO COMPLETE GOAL:

Anticipated Completion Date:

Possible Road Blocks:

WEEKLY GOAL DIGGER TRACKER

Weekly Priorities:

Weekly Checklist:

Notes:

WEEKLY GOAL DIGGER TRACKER

Week

Monday

Tuesday

Wednesday

Thursday

Friday

Saturday

Sunday

	Monday	Tuesday	Wednesday	Thursday	Friday	Saturday	Sunday
6:30am							
7:00am							
7:30am							
8:00am							
8:30am							
9:00am							
9:30am							
10:00am							
10:30am							
11:00am							
11:30am							
12:00pm							
12:30pm							
1:00pm							
1:30pm							
2:00pm							
2:30pm							
3:00pm							
3:30pm							
4:00pm							
4:30pm							
5:00pm							
5:30pm							
6:00pm							

	Monday	Tuesday	Wednesday	Thursday	Friday	Saturday	Sunday
6:30pm							
7:00pm							
7:30pm							
8:00pm							
8:30pm							
9:00pm							
9:30pm							
10:00pm							
10:30pm							

GOAL TRACKER PLAN SHEET

Goal :

Motivation/Reward:

Start Date: _____   Goal Completion Date: _____

Duration? How long will it take? _____

ACTION PLAN

STEPS NEEDED TO COMPLETE GOAL:

Anticipated Completion Date:

Possible Road Blocks:

WEEKLY GOAL DIGGER TRACKER

Weekly Priorities:

Weekly Checklist:

Notes:

WEEKLY GOAL DIGGER TRACKER

Week

Monday

Tuesday

Wednesday

Thursday

Friday

Saturday

Sunday

	Monday	Tuesday	Wednesday	Thursday	Friday	Saturday	Sunday
6:30am							
7:00am							
7:30am							
8:00am							
8:30am							
9:00am							
9:30am							
10:00am							
10:30am							
11:00am							
11:30am							
12:00pm							
12:30pm							
1:00pm							
1:30pm							
2:00pm							
2:30pm							
3:00pm							
3:30pm							
4:00pm							
4:30pm							
5:00pm							
5:30pm							
6:00pm							

	Monday	Tuesday	Wednesday	Thursday	Friday	Saturday	Sunday
6:30pm							
7:00pm							
7:30pm							
8:00pm							
8:30pm							
9:00pm							
9:30pm							
10:00pm							
10:30pm							

GOAL TRACKER PLAN SHEET

Goal:

Motivation/Reward:

Start Date: _____ Goal Completion Date: _____

Duration? How long will it take? _____

ACTION PLAN

STEPS NEEDED TO COMPLETE GOAL:

Anticipated Completion Date:

Possible Road Blocks:

WEEKLY GOAL DIGGER TRACKER

Weekly Priorities:

Weekly Checklist:

Notes:

WEEKLY GOAL DIGGER TRACKER

Week

Monday

Tuesday

Wednesday

Thursday

Friday

Saturday

Sunday

	Monday	Tuesday	Wednesday	Thursday	Friday	Saturday	Sunday
6:30am							
7:00am							
7:30am							
8:00am							
8:30am							
9:00am							
9:30am							
10:00am							
10:30am							
11:00am							
11:30am							
12:00pm							
12:30pm							
1:00pm							
1:30pm							
2:00pm							
2:30pm							
3:00pm							
3:30pm							
4:00pm							
4:30pm							
5:00pm							
5:30pm							
6:00pm							

	Monday	Tuesday	Wednesday	Thursday	Friday	Saturday	Sunday
6:30pm							
7:00pm							
7:30pm							
8:00pm							
8:30pm							
9:00pm							
9:30pm							
10:00pm							
10:30pm							

Sunday	Monday	Tuesday	Wednesday	Thursday	Friday	Saturday

Goal Digger Workbook

Goal Overview

Analyze each goal by doing a Tracker Planner Sheet for each Goal

GOAL TRACKER PLAN SHEET

Goal :

Motivation/Reward:

Start Date: _____   Goal Completion Date: _____

Duration? How long will it take? _____

ACTION PLAN

STEPS NEEDED TO COMPLETE GOAL:

Anticipated Completion Date:

Possible Road Blocks:

Analyze each goal by doing a Tracker Planner Sheet for each Goal

GOAL TRACKER PLAN SHEET
Goal :
Motivation/Reward:

Start Date: _____ Goal Completion Date: _____

Duration? How long will it take? _____

ACTION PLAN
STEPS NEEDED TO COMPLETE GOAL:
Anticipated Completion Date:
Possible Road Blocks:

GOAL TRACKER PLAN SHEET

Goal :

Motivation/Reward:

Start Date: _____ Goal Completion Date: _____

Duration? How long will it take? _____

ACTION PLAN

STEPS NEEDED TO COMPLETE GOAL:

Anticipated Completion Date:

Possible Road Blocks:

WEEKLY GOAL DIGGER TRACKER

Weekly Priorities:

Weekly Checklist:

Notes:

WEEKLY GOAL DIGGER TRACKER

Week

Monday

Tuesday

Wednesday

Thursday

Friday

Saturday

Sunday

	Monday	Tuesday	Wednesday	Thursday	Friday	Saturday	Sunday
6:30am							
7:00am							
7:30am							
8:00am							
8:30am							
9:00am							
9:30am							
10:00am							
10:30am							
11:00am							
11:30am							
12:00pm							
12:30pm							
1:00pm							
1:30pm							
2:00pm							
2:30pm							
3:00pm							
3:30pm							
4:00pm							
4:30pm							
5:00pm							
5:30pm							
6:00pm							

	Monday	Tuesday	Wednesday	Thursday	Friday	Saturday	Sunday
6:30pm							
7:00pm							
7:30pm							
8:00pm							
8:30pm							
9:00pm							
9:30pm							
10:00pm							
10:30pm							

BOSS CHICK

GOAL TRACKER PLAN SHEET

Goal:

Motivation/Reward:

Start Date: _____ Goal Completion Date: _____

Duration? How long will it take? _____

ACTION PLAN

STEPS NEEDED TO COMPLETE GOAL:

Anticipated Completion Date:

Possible Road Blocks:

WEEKLY GOAL DIGGER TRACKER

Weekly Priorities:

Weekly Checklist:

Notes:

WEEKLY GOAL DIGGER TRACKER

Week

Monday

Tuesday

Wednesday

Thursday

Friday

Saturday

Sunday

	Monday	Tuesday	Wednesday	Thursday	Friday	Saturday	Sunday
6:30am							
7:00am							
7:30am							
8:00am							
8:30am							
9:00am							
9:30am							
10:00am							
10:30am							
11:00am							
11:30am							
12:00pm							
12:30pm							
1:00pm							
1:30pm							
2:00pm							
2:30pm							
3:00pm							
3:30pm							
4:00pm							
4:30pm							
5:00pm							
5:30pm							
6:00pm							

	Monday	Tuesday	Wednesday	Thursday	Friday	Saturday	Sunday
6:30pm							
7:00pm							
7:30pm							
8:00pm							
8:30pm							
9:00pm							
9:30pm							
10:00pm							
10:30pm							

GOAL TRACKER PLAN SHEET

Goal :

Motivation/Reward:

Start Date: _____ Goal Completion Date: _____

Duration? How long will it take? _____

ACTION PLAN

STEPS NEEDED TO COMPLETE GOAL:

Anticipated Completion Date:

Possible Road Blocks:

WEEKLY GOAL DIGGER TRACKER

Weekly Priorities:

Weekly Checklist:

Notes:

WEEKLY GOAL DIGGER TRACKER

Week

Monday

Tuesday

Wednesday

Thursday

Friday

Saturday

Sunday

	Monday	Tuesday	Wednesday	Thursday	Friday	Saturday	Sunday
6:30am							
7:00am							
7:30am							
8:00am							
8:30am							
9:00am							
9:30am							
10:00am							
10:30am							
11:00am							
11:30am							
12:00pm							
12:30pm							
1:00pm							
1:30pm							
2:00pm							
2:30pm							
3:00pm							
3:30pm							
4:00pm							
4:30pm							
5:00pm							
5:30pm							
6:00pm							

	Monday	Tuesday	Wednesday	Thursday	Friday	Saturday	Sunday
6:30pm							
7:00pm							
7:30pm							
8:00pm							
8:30pm							
9:00pm							
9:30pm							
10:00pm							
10:30pm							

GOAL TRACKER PLAN SHEET

Goal :

Motivation/Reward:

Start Date: _____   Goal Completion Date: _____

Duration? How long will it take? _____

ACTION PLAN

STEPS NEEDED TO COMPLETE GOAL:

Anticipated Completion Date:

Possible Road Blocks:

WEEKLY GOAL DIGGER TRACKER

Weekly Priorities:

Weekly Checklist:

Notes:

WEEKLY GOAL DIGGER TRACKER

Week

Monday

Tuesday

Wednesday

Thursday

Friday

Saturday

Sunday

	Monday	Tuesday	Wednesday	Thursday	Friday	Saturday	Sunday
6:30am							
7:00am							
7:30am							
8:00am							
8:30am							
9:00am							
9:30am							
10:00am							
10:30am							
11:00am							
11:30am							
12:00pm							
12:30pm							
1:00pm							
1:30pm							
2:00pm							
2:30pm							
3:00pm							
3:30pm							
4:00pm							
4:30pm							
5:00pm							
5:30pm							
6:00pm							

	Monday	Tuesday	Wednesday	Thursday	Friday	Saturday	Sunday
6:30pm							
7:00pm							
7:30pm							
8:00pm							
8:30pm							
9:00pm							
9:30pm							
10:00pm							
10:30pm							

Sunday	Monday	Tuesday	Wednesday	Thursday	Friday	Saturday

Goal Digger Workbook

Goal Overview

Analyze each goal by doing a Tracker Planner Sheet for each Goal

GOAL TRACKER PLAN SHEET

Goal:

Motivation/Reward:

Start Date: _____   Goal Completion Date: _____

Duration? How long will it take? _____

ACTION PLAN

STEPS NEEDED TO COMPLETE GOAL:

Anticipated Completion Date:

Possible Road Blocks:

Analyze each goal by doing a Tracker Planner Sheet for each Goal

GOAL TRACKER PLAN SHEET

Goal:

Motivation/Reward:

Start Date: _____   Goal Completion Date: _____

Duration? How long will it take? _____

ACTION PLAN

STEPS NEEDED TO COMPLETE GOAL:

Anticipated Completion Date:

Possible Road Blocks:

GOAL TRACKER PLAN SHEET

Goal :

Motivation/Reward:

Start Date: _____ Goal Completion Date: _____

Duration? How long will it take? _____

ACTION PLAN

STEPS NEEDED TO COMPLETE GOAL:

Anticipated Completion Date:

Possible Road Blocks:

WEEKLY GOAL DIGGER TRACKER

Weekly Priorities:

Weekly Checklist:

Notes:

WEEKLY GOAL DIGGER TRACKER

Week

Monday

Tuesday

Wednesday

Thursday

Friday

Saturday

Sunday

	Monday	Tuesday	Wednesday	Thursday	Friday	Saturday	Sunday
6:30am							
7:00am							
7:30am							
8:00am							
8:30am							
9:00am							
9:30am							
10:00am							
10:30am							
11:00am							
11:30am							
12:00pm							
12:30pm							
1:00pm							
1:30pm							
2:00pm							
2:30pm							
3:00pm							
3:30pm							
4:00pm							
4:30pm							
5:00pm							
5:30pm							
6:00pm							

	Monday	Tuesday	Wednesday	Thursday	Friday	Saturday	Sunday
6:30pm							
7:00pm							
7:30pm							
8:00pm							
8:30pm							
9:00pm							
9:30pm							
10:00pm							
10:30pm							

GOAL TRACKER PLAN SHEET

Goal :

Motivation/Reward:

Start Date: _____ Goal Completion Date: _____

Duration? How long will it take? _____

ACTION PLAN

STEPS NEEDED TO COMPLETE GOAL:

Anticipated Completion Date:

Possible Road Blocks:

WEEKLY GOAL DIGGER TRACKER

Weekly Priorities:

Weekly Checklist:

Notes:

WEEKLY GOAL DIGGER TRACKER

Week

Monday

Tuesday

Wednesday

Thursday

Friday

Saturday

Sunday

	Monday	Tuesday	Wednesday	Thursday	Friday	Saturday	Sunday
6:30am							
7:00am							
7:30am							
8:00am							
8:30am							
9:00am							
9:30am							
10:00am							
10:30am							
11:00am							
11:30am							
12:00pm							
12:30pm							
1:00pm							
1:30pm							
2:00pm							
2:30pm							
3:00pm							
3:30pm							
4:00pm							
4:30pm							
5:00pm							
5:30pm							
6:00pm							

	Monday	Tuesday	Wednesday	Thursday	Friday	Saturday	Sunday
6:30pm							
7:00pm							
7:30pm							
8:00pm							
8:30pm							
9:00pm							
9:30pm							
10:00pm							
10:30pm							

GOAL TRACKER PLAN SHEET

Goal :

Motivation/Reward:

Start Date: _____ Goal Completion Date: _____

Duration? How long will it take? _____

ACTION PLAN

STEPS NEEDED TO COMPLETE GOAL:

Anticipated Completion Date:

Possible Road Blocks:

137

WEEKLY GOAL DIGGER TRACKER

Weekly Priorities:

Weekly Checklist:

Notes:

WEEKLY GOAL DIGGER TRACKER

Week

Monday

Tuesday

Wednesday

Thursday

Friday

Saturday

Sunday

	Monday	Tuesday	Wednesday	Thursday	Friday	Saturday	Sunday
6:30am							
7:00am							
7:30am							
8:00am							
8:30am							
9:00am							
9:30am							
10:00am							
10:30am							
11:00am							
11:30am							
12:00pm							
12:30pm							
1:00pm							
1:30pm							
2:00pm							
2:30pm							
3:00pm							
3:30pm							
4:00pm							
4:30pm							
5:00pm							
5:30pm							
6:00pm							

	Monday	Tuesday	Wednesday	Thursday	Friday	Saturday	Sunday
6:30pm							
7:00pm							
7:30pm							
8:00pm							
8:30pm							
9:00pm							
9:30pm							
10:00pm							
10:30pm							

GOAL TRACKER PLAN SHEET

Goal :

Motivation/Reward:

Start Date: _____   Goal Completion Date: _____

Duration? How long will it take? _____

ACTION PLAN

STEPS NEEDED TO COMPLETE GOAL:

Anticipated Completion Date:

Possible Road Blocks:

WEEKLY GOAL DIGGER TRACKER

Weekly Priorities:

Weekly Checklist:

Notes:

WEEKLY GOAL DIGGER TRACKER

Week

Monday

Tuesday

Wednesday

Thursday

Friday

Saturday

Sunday

	Monday	Tuesday	Wednesday	Thursday	Friday	Saturday	Sunday
6:30am							
7:00am							
7:30am							
8:00am							
8:30am							
9:00am							
9:30am							
10:00am							
10:30am							
11:00am							
11:30am							
12:00pm							
12:30pm							
1:00pm							
1:30pm							
2:00pm							
2:30pm							
3:00pm							
3:30pm							
4:00pm							
4:30pm							
5:00pm							
5:30pm							
6:00pm							

	Monday	Tuesday	Wednesday	Thursday	Friday	Saturday	Sunday
6:30pm							
7:00pm							
7:30pm							
8:00pm							
8:30pm							
9:00pm							
9:30pm							
10:00pm							
10:30pm							

Sunday	Monday	Tuesday	Wednesday	Thursday	Friday	Saturday

Goal Digger Workbook

Goal Overview

Analyze each goal by doing a Tracker Planner Sheet for each Goal

GOAL TRACKER PLAN SHEET
Goal:
Motivation/Reward:

Start Date: _____   Goal Completion Date: _____

Duration? How long will it take? _____

ACTION PLAN
STEPS NEEDED TO COMPLETE GOAL:
Anticipated Completion Date:
Possible Road Blocks:

Analyze each goal by doing a Tracker Planner Sheet for each Goal

GOAL TRACKER PLAN SHEET

Goal:

Motivation/Reward:

Start Date: _____   Goal Completion Date: _____

Duration? How long will it take? _____

ACTION PLAN

STEPS NEEDED TO COMPLETE GOAL:

Anticipated Completion Date:

Possible Road Blocks:

GOAL TRACKER PLAN SHEET

Goal:

Motivation/Reward:

Start Date: _____ Goal Completion Date: _____

Duration? How long will it take? _____

ACTION PLAN

STEPS NEEDED TO COMPLETE GOAL:

Anticipated Completion Date:

Possible Road Blocks:

WEEKLY GOAL DIGGER TRACKER

Weekly Priorities:

Weekly Checklist:

Notes:

WEEKLY GOAL DIGGER TRACKER

Week

Monday

Tuesday

Wednesday

Thursday

Friday

Saturday

Sunday

	Monday	Tuesday	Wednesday	Thursday	Friday	Saturday	Sunday
6:30am							
7:00am							
7:30am							
8:00am							
8:30am							
9:00am							
9:30am							
10:00am							
10:30am							
11:00am							
11:30am							
12:00pm							
12:30pm							
1:00pm							
1:30pm							
2:00pm							
2:30pm							
3:00pm							
3:30pm							
4:00pm							
4:30pm							
5:00pm							
5:30pm							
6:00pm							

	Monday	Tuesday	Wednesday	Thursday	Friday	Saturday	Sunday
6:30pm							
7:00pm							
7:30pm							
8:00pm							
8:30pm							
9:00pm							
9:30pm							
10:00pm							
10:30pm							

GOAL TRACKER PLAN SHEET

Goal :

Motivation/Reward:

Start Date: _____   Goal Completion Date: _____

Duration? How long will it take? _____

ACTION PLAN

STEPS NEEDED TO COMPLETE GOAL:

Anticipated Completion Date:

Possible Road Blocks:

WEEKLY GOAL DIGGER TRACKER

Weekly Priorities:

Weekly Checklist:

Notes:

WEEKLY GOAL DIGGER TRACKER

Week	
Monday	
Tuesday	
Wednesday	
Thursday	
Friday	
Saturday	
Sunday	

	Monday	Tuesday	Wednesday	Thursday	Friday	Saturday	Sunday
6:30am							
7:00am							
7:30am							
8:00am							
8:30am							
9:00am							
9:30am							
10:00am							
10:30am							
11:00am							
11:30am							
12:00pm							
12:30pm							
1:00pm							
1:30pm							
2:00pm							
2:30pm							
3:00pm							
3:30pm							
4:00pm							
4:30pm							
5:00pm							
5:30pm							
6:00pm							

	Monday	Tuesday	Wednesday	Thursday	Friday	Saturday	Sunday
6:30pm							
7:00pm							
7:30pm							
8:00pm							
8:30pm							
9:00pm							
9:30pm							
10:00pm							
10:30pm							

GOAL TRACKER PLAN SHEET

Goal :

Motivation/Reward:

Start Date: _____   Goal Completion Date: _____

Duration? How long will it take? _____

ACTION PLAN

STEPS NEEDED TO COMPLETE GOAL:

Anticipated Completion Date:

Possible Road Blocks:

WEEKLY GOAL DIGGER TRACKER

Weekly Priorities:

Weekly Checklist:

Notes:

WEEKLY GOAL DIGGER TRACKER

Week

Monday

Tuesday

Wednesday

Thursday

Friday

Saturday

Sunday

	Monday	Tuesday	Wednesday	Thursday	Friday	Saturday	Sunday
6:30am							
7:00am							
7:30am							
8:00am							
8:30am							
9:00am							
9:30am							
10:00am							
10:30am							
11:00am							
11:30am							
12:00pm							
12:30pm							
1:00pm							
1:30pm							
2:00pm							
2:30pm							
3:00pm							
3:30pm							
4:00pm							
4:30pm							
5:00pm							
5:30pm							
6:00pm							

	Monday	Tuesday	Wednesday	Thursday	Friday	Saturday	Sunday
6:30pm							
7:00pm							
7:30pm							
8:00pm							
8:30pm							
9:00pm							
9:30pm							
10:00pm							
10:30pm							

GOAL TRACKER PLAN SHEET

Goal :

Motivation/Reward:

Start Date: _____   Goal Completion Date: _____

Duration? How long will it take? _____

ACTION PLAN

STEPS NEEDED TO COMPLETE GOAL:

Anticipated Completion Date:

Possible Road Blocks:

WEEKLY GOAL DIGGER TRACKER

Weekly Priorities:

Weekly Checklist:

Notes:

WEEKLY GOAL DIGGER TRACKER

Week

Monday

Tuesday

Wednesday

Thursday

Friday

Saturday

Sunday

	Monday	Tuesday	Wednesday	Thursday	Friday	Saturday	Sunday
6:30am							
7:00am							
7:30am							
8:00am							
8:30am							
9:00am							
9:30am							
10:00am							
10:30am							
11:00am							
11:30am							
12:00pm							
12:30pm							
1:00pm							
1:30pm							
2:00pm							
2:30pm							
3:00pm							
3:30pm							
4:00pm							
4:30pm							
5:00pm							
5:30pm							
6:00pm							

	Monday	Tuesday	Wednesday	Thursday	Friday	Saturday	Sunday
6:30pm							
7:00pm							
7:30pm							
8:00pm							
8:30pm							
9:00pm							
9:30pm							
10:00pm							
10:30pm							

Sunday	Monday	Tuesday	Wednesday	Thursday	Friday	Saturday

Goal Digger Workbook

Goal Overview

Analyze each goal by doing a Tracker Planner Sheet for each Goal

---

GOAL TRACKER PLAN SHEET

Goal:

Motivation/Reward:

Start Date: _____   Goal Completion Date: _____

Duration? How long will it take? _____

ACTION PLAN

STEPS NEEDED TO COMPLETE GOAL:

Anticipated Completion Date:

Possible Road Blocks:

Analyze each goal by doing a Tracker Planner Sheet for each Goal

GOAL TRACKER PLAN SHEET
Goal:
Motivation/Reward:

Start Date: _____ Goal Completion Date: _____

Duration? How long will it take? _____

ACTION PLAN
STEPS NEEDED TO COMPLETE GOAL:
Anticipated Completion Date:
Possible Road Blocks:

GOAL TRACKER PLAN SHEET

Goal :

Motivation/Reward:

Start Date: _____   Goal Completion Date: _____

Duration? How long will it take? _____

ACTION PLAN

STEPS NEEDED TO COMPLETE GOAL:

Anticipated Completion Date:

Possible Road Blocks:

WEEKLY GOAL DIGGER TRACKER

Weekly Priorities:

Weekly Checklist:

Notes:

WEEKLY GOAL DIGGER TRACKER

Week

Monday

Tuesday

Wednesday

Thursday

Friday

Saturday

Sunday

	Monday	Tuesday	Wednesday	Thursday	Friday	Saturday	Sunday
6:30am							
7:00am							
7:30am							
8:00am							
8:30am							
9:00am							
9:30am							
10:00am							
10:30am							
11:00am							
11:30am							
12:00pm							
12:30pm							
1:00pm							
1:30pm							
2:00pm							
2:30pm							
3:00pm							
3:30pm							
4:00pm							
4:30pm							
5:00pm							
5:30pm							
6:00pm							

	Monday	Tuesday	Wednesday	Thursday	Friday	Saturday	Sunday
6:30pm							
7:00pm							
7:30pm							
8:00pm							
8:30pm							
9:00pm							
9:30pm							
10:00pm							
10:30pm							

GOAL TRACKER PLAN SHEET

Goal :

Motivation/Reward:

Start Date: _____ Goal Completion Date: _____

Duration? How long will it take? _____

ACTION PLAN

STEPS NEEDED TO COMPLETE GOAL:

Anticipated Completion Date:

Possible Road Blocks:

WEEKLY GOAL DIGGER TRACKER

Weekly Priorities:

Weekly Checklist:

Notes:

WEEKLY GOAL DIGGER TRACKER

Week

Monday

Tuesday

Wednesday

Thursday

Friday

Saturday

Sunday

	Monday	Tuesday	Wednesday	Thursday	Friday	Saturday	Sunday
6:30am							
7:00am							
7:30am							
8:00am							
8:30am							
9:00am							
9:30am							
10:00am							
10:30am							
11:00am							
11:30am							
12:00pm							
12:30pm							
1:00pm							
1:30pm							
2:00pm							
2:30pm							
3:00pm							
3:30pm							
4:00pm							
4:30pm							
5:00pm							
5:30pm							
6:00pm							

	Monday	Tuesday	Wednesday	Thursday	Friday	Saturday	Sunday
6:30pm							
7:00pm							
7:30pm							
8:00pm							
8:30pm							
9:00pm							
9:30pm							
10:00pm							
10:30pm							

GOAL TRACKER PLAN SHEET

Goal :

Motivation/Reward:

Start Date: _____   Goal Completion Date: _____

Duration? How long will it take? _____

ACTION PLAN

STEPS NEEDED TO COMPLETE GOAL:

Anticipated Completion Date:

Possible Road Blocks:

WEEKLY GOAL DIGGER TRACKER

Weekly Priorities:

Weekly Checklist:

Notes:

WEEKLY GOAL DIGGER TRACKER

Week

Monday

Tuesday

Wednesday

Thursday

Friday

Saturday

Sunday

	Monday	Tuesday	Wednesday	Thursday	Friday	Saturday	Sunday
6:30am							
7:00am							
7:30am							
8:00am							
8:30am							
9:00am							
9:30am							
10:00am							
10:30am							
11:00am							
11:30am							
12:00pm							
12:30pm							
1:00pm							
1:30pm							
2:00pm							
2:30pm							
3:00pm							
3:30pm							
4:00pm							
4:30pm							
5:00pm							
5:30pm							
6:00pm							

	Monday	Tuesday	Wednesday	Thursday	Friday	Saturday	Sunday
6:30pm							
7:00pm							
7:30pm							
8:00pm							
8:30pm							
9:00pm							
9:30pm							
10:00pm							
10:30pm							

GOAL TRACKER PLAN SHEET

Goal :

Motivation/Reward:

Start Date: _____   Goal Completion Date: _____

Duration? How long will it take? _____

ACTION PLAN

STEPS NEEDED TO COMPLETE GOAL:

Anticipated Completion Date:

Possible Road Blocks:

WEEKLY GOAL DIGGER TRACKER

Weekly Priorities:

Weekly Checklist:

Notes:

WEEKLY GOAL DIGGER TRACKER

Week

Monday

Tuesday

Wednesday

Thursday

Friday

Saturday

Sunday

	Monday	Tuesday	Wednesday	Thursday	Friday	Saturday	Sunday
6:30am							
7:00am							
7:30am							
8:00am							
8:30am							
9:00am							
9:30am							
10:00am							
10:30am							
11:00am							
11:30am							
12:00pm							
12:30pm							
1:00pm							
1:30pm							
2:00pm							
2:30pm							
3:00pm							
3:30pm							
4:00pm							
4:30pm							
5:00pm							
5:30pm							
6:00pm							

	Monday	Tuesday	Wednesday	Thursday	Friday	Saturday	Sunday
6:30pm							
7:00pm							
7:30pm							
8:00pm							
8:30pm							
9:00pm							
9:30pm							
10:00pm							
10:30pm							

Boss Rule # 5

DOMINATING MONEY TO SUPPORT YOUR GOALS

Plan your finances

"Become so financially secure that you forget its payday"

"Money helps you have more options"

BOSS CHICK

☞ THE BOSS BUDGET Saving Plan ☜

Budget GOAL:	MONTH:

Think about the Top 10 Ways to Save

List different types of ways that you can save (example: Savings Account, saving $1.00 bills only, saving change, putting an amount in your saving or bank account and etc.)

1. _____
2. _____
3. _____
4. _____
5. _____
6. _____
7. _____
8. _____
9. _____
10. _____

THE BOSS BUDGET Saving Plan

MOTIVATION/REWARD:
GOAL:

START DATE: _____ GOAL COMPLETION DATE: _____

(DURATION) HOW LONG WILL IT TAKE? _____

ACTION PLAN:
STEPS NEEDED TO COMPLETE GOAL
ANTICIPATED COMPLETION DATE:
POSSIBLE ROAD BLOCKS:

Notes:

_____

_____

_____

Monthly Budget Tracker: Fixed Expenses

These are expenses that remain the same every month (Rent, Mortgage, Property Taxes, Utility Bills, Car Loan Payments, Car Insurance, Life insurance, Set Debt Payments)

Bill	Due Date	Projected Amount	Actual Amount
Rent/Mortgage			
Electricity			
Gas			
Water/Trash Removal			
Vehicle Payment			
Gas/Transportation			
Groceries			
Phone			
Internet/Cable			
Loan Payment Car/Student Loan Etc			
Entertainment			
Personal			
Medical			
Pet			
Credit Card			
Emergency Fund Savings			
	Total		

SPENDING TRACKER......

DATE	ITEM	Amount
		TOTAL

Bill	AMOUNT
Rent/Mortgage	
Electricity	
Gas	
Water/Trash Removal	
Vehicle Payment	
Gas/Transportation	
Groceries	
Phone	
Internet/Cable	
Loan Payment Car/Student Loan Etc	
Entertainment	
Personal	
Medical	
Pet	
Credit Card	
Emergency Fund Savings	
	Total

TALLYING UP YOUR BOSS SPENDING

	BUDGETED	ACTUAL	DIFFERENCE
TOTAL Expenses			

Income	Expenses	DIFFERENCE
$	$	

Are you In the Red or Green?

Review your current situation BASED on the Money spent on your Spending Tracker

What types of items did you spend the most money on?

What ways can you cut cost?

What are some things that you can eliminate?

<u>Set some spending GOALS for the next Month</u>

1.
2.
3.
4.
5.

THE BOSS BUDGET PLANNING SHEET

Budget GOAL:	MONTH:

INCOME BREAKDOWN
ANY EXPECTED AMOUNT OF MONEY YOU RECEIVE
from employment, contracts, loans or gifts

DATE	DESCRIPTION INCOME SOURCE	AMOUNT	AFTER TAXES

Fixed Expenses
These are expenses that remain the same every month
(Rent, Mortgage, Property Taxes, Utility Bills, Car Loan Payments,
Car Insurance, Life insurance, Set Debt Payments)

Due Date	Description	Amount
	Total	

Other Expenses
You can include:

Groceries | Work Lunches | Netflix
Fuel | Snacks | Parking
Entertainment | Clothing & Shoes | Lottery
Hair | Hobbies | Beauty Budget
Pet Food/Bills | Day Care | Clubs or Dues

Due Date	Description	Amount
	Total	

TALLYING UP YOUR BOSS EXPENSES

	BUDGETED	ACTUAL	DIFFERENCE
TOTAL Expenses			

Income	Expenses	DIFFERENCE
$	$	

Are you In the Red or Green?

Review your current situation

Are you in the Red or Green?

_____

What areas do you need to cut cost?

MONEY TALK

Lets Talk about Saving Money as an option to general extra money:

Think about Saving Ideas:

What method should you commit to?

_____

_____

Goal Amount for Saving $

_____

How do you plan to cut cost?
(List Below)

Generating Money with a Hustle & a Start Up Plan

Name a few things that you can do to start generate extra money:

_____

_____

What do you need to do to get started?

1. _____
2. _____
3. _____
4. _____
5. _____
6. _____
7. _____
8. _____

How much money you plan to make a week $_____

How much money you plan to make a month $_____

How much money you plan to make a year $_____

What do you plan to do?

How do you plan on doing it? (Complete a Goal Tracker Sheet for your new venture)

THE GOAL TRACKER PLAN SHEET

MOTIVATION/REWARD:
GOAL:

START DATE: _____ GOAL COMPLETION DATE: _____

(DURATION) HOW LONG WILL IT TAKE? _____

ACTION PLAN:
STEPS NEEDED TO COMPLETE GOAL
ANTICIPATED COMPLETION DATE:
POSSIBLE ROAD BLOCKS:

GOAL DIGGIN

Creating your GOAL BOARD

"Without a plan every goal is just a wish"

Important Fact:
Goal Boards are very different from Vision Boards
Goal Boards are very specific and time sensitive
Goal Boards require you to create a monthly checklist of
what is needed to help you complete your goals
Goal Boards allow you to see you progress and keep your goals
in line by prioritizing the process of completing them

"When you don't plan you plan to fail"

Materials for your GOAL BOARD EXPERIENCE:

Plain Board 22in x 28in or the size that best suits you

Post It Sticky Notes 3in x 3in – 5 Pack preferably different colors

1. Black Marker Any Desirable Size
2. Ruler
3. Poster Board Boarder for the Ends of your Board
4. Glue
5. Tape
6. Write the months of the year on one sticky note (This will be used later to draft your goal board)

January, February, March, April, May, June, July, August, September, October, November, December

How to create your Goal Board!

Step 1: Brainstorm
Use Each Color Sticky Note as a Topic

What are some areas of your life that you would like to focus on?

Think about all areas it could be Business, Personal, Spiritual, Mental (other examples: Financial, Healthy Lifestyle, Eating, Family, Travel,)
List them below using the sticky note numbers 1-5

Sticky Note 1: _____

Sticky Note 2: _____

Sticky Note 3: _____

Sticky Note 4: _____

Sticky Note 5: _____

After you write a TOPIC on the top of each stack of sticky notes
move to the next step Determining your goals

Decorate your Board

You can decide to put your boarder around your board at this time, Put your months on the Board

(It is suggested to do 3-6 months on your board at a time)

You can also decorate and be as creative as you like to make your board as desirable as you prefer

Step 2: Brainstorm by determining your Goals

Take a couple minutes on each stack of sticky notes and focus on one
topic at a time. Give yourself about 2 minutes on each topic

Write one goal on each stick note

Start with the stack that you listed as #1

Without thinking too hard take Sticky Note Stack #1 and flip up the first sticky note with the topic on the front and write on the second sticky note something that you would like to do to improve in this area. You can also write goals you would like to complete in that area as well.

After completing Topic #1 with the first stack of sticky notes Continue with Brainstorming by

Picking up the second sticky note stack listed as #2 on your paper Flip to the next sticky note in stack #2 and write one goal on each sticky note be sure to only write goals from this category

(you will have time to write goals regarding other categories with the other sticky note topics)

Proceed to Sticky Note Stack #3 and repeat until you have
completed all 5 topics and wrote notes on all 5 topics

Note: You do not need to necessarily have 5 topics or use every sticky note in every stack

Lets Draft Your Goal Board

Step 3: Once you have completed your Sticky Note Stacks you are ready to draft your board

Start with one sticky note stack and with each Goal stick it on the month that you
feel is most realistic to complete it and continue until all the sticky notes has all
been properly placed. Some goals way be realistic to do in the current month and
others may take a while. Remember to make and organize SMART GOALS.

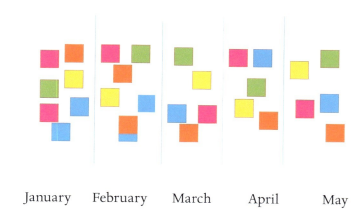

January   February   March   April   May

Each color square represents a different Goal Topic

You can put as many as you need to in one month from any topic.

Step 4: Now that you have completed your goal board you want to post it somewhere that is visible and in a place that will force you to look at it on a daily basis.

Personal Bathroom, Room, Closet, Makeup Room, Living Room

Dinner Room Etc.

Goal Board Suggestions

As you complete your goals you should remove them and place them in a container

This will help track success and remind you to celebrate on how far you have come

It is important to look at your goal board daily and to use this Goal Book as a Guide on a daily basis to ensure that you are accomplishing your goals to their full potential

Boss Notes:

Boss Notes:

Boss Notes:

_____

_____

_____

_____

_____

_____

_____

_____

_____

_____

_____

_____

_____

Boss Notes:

_____

_____

_____

_____

_____

_____

_____

_____

_____

_____

_____

_____

_____

Printed in the United States
By Bookmasters